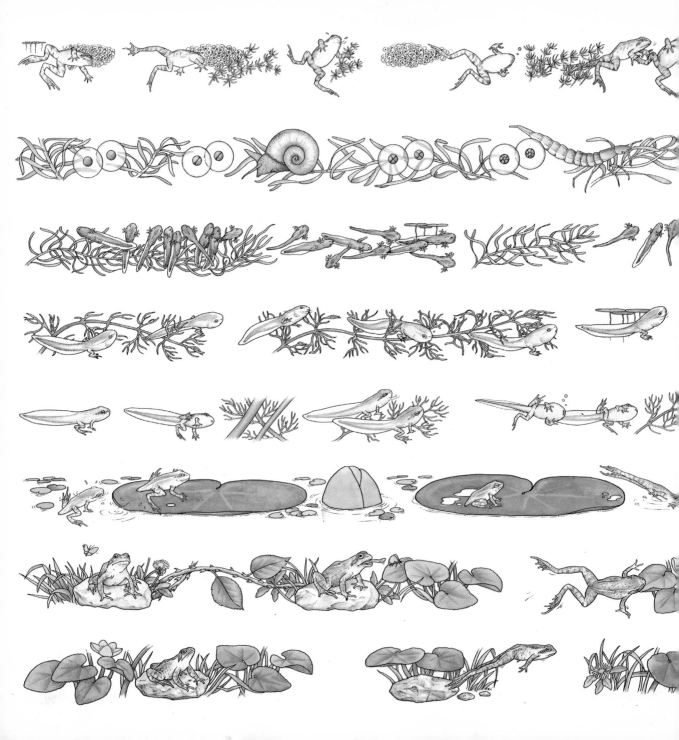

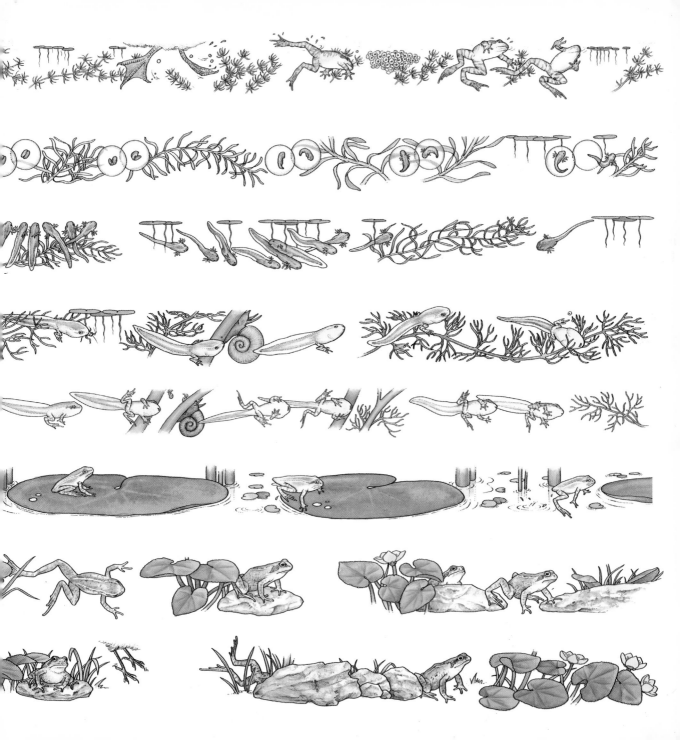

Dorling **DK** Kindersley

LONDON, NEW YORK, SYDNEY, DELHI, PARIS, MUNICH, AND JOHANNESBURG

Written and edited by Angela Royston
Art Editor Nigel Hazle
Production Marguerite Fenn
Illustrators Sandra Pond and Will Giles

First American Edition, 2001

00 01 02 03 04 05 10 9 8 7 6 5 4 3 2 1

Published in the United States by Dorling Kindersley Publishing, Inc.
95 Madison Avenue, New York, New York 10016

A CIP catalog record for this book is available
from the Library of Congress

ISBN 0-7894-7656-8

Color reproduction by Scantrans, Singapore
Printed and bound in Italy by L.E.G.O.

See our complete
catalog at

www.dk.com

SEE HOW THEY GROW
FROG

photographed by
KIM TAYLOR
and JANE BURTON

A DORLING KINDERSLEY BOOK

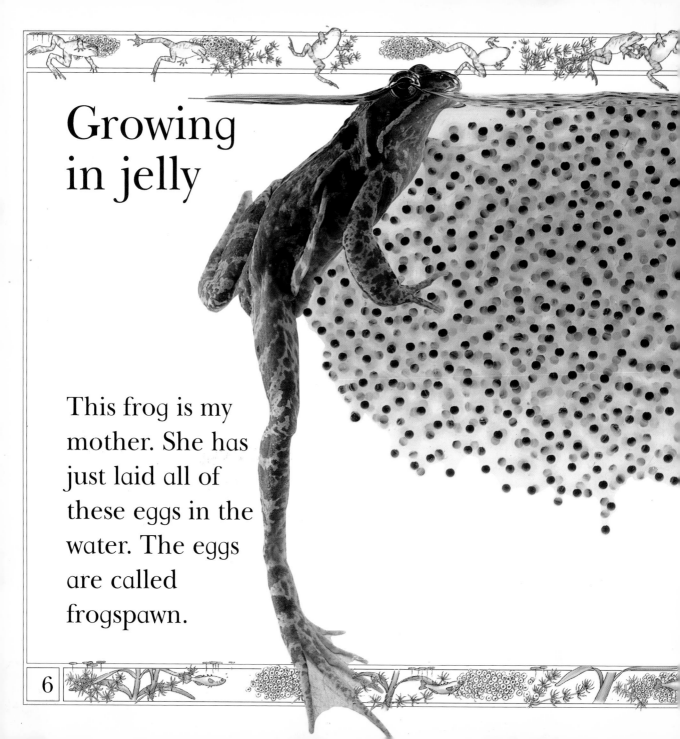

Growing in jelly

This frog is my mother. She has just laid all of these eggs in the water. The eggs are called frogspawn.

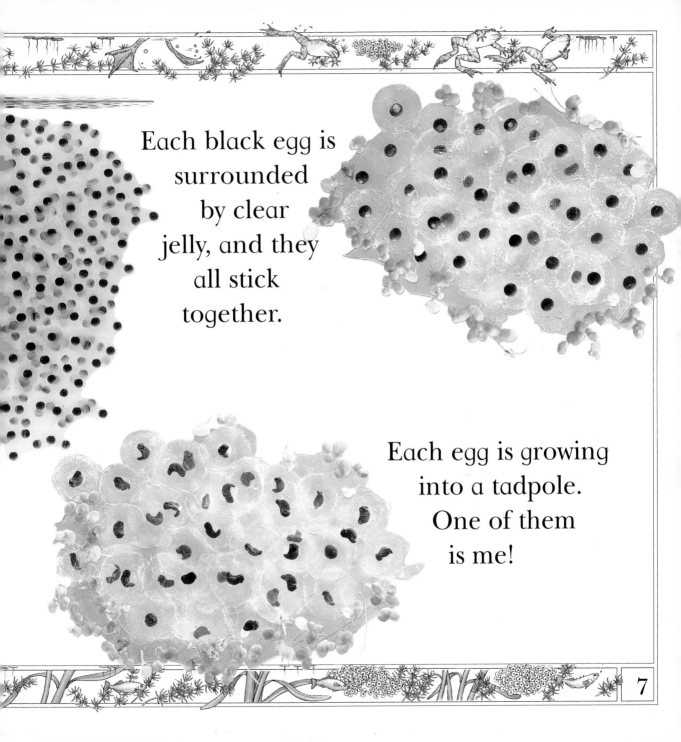

Each black egg is
surrounded
by clear
jelly, and they
all stick
together.

Each egg is growing
into a tadpole.
One of them
is me!

Just hatched

After two weeks I
am ready to hatch.

Look at my long
feathery gills. They let
me breathe underwater.

I push my way
through the
frogspawn and
swim away.

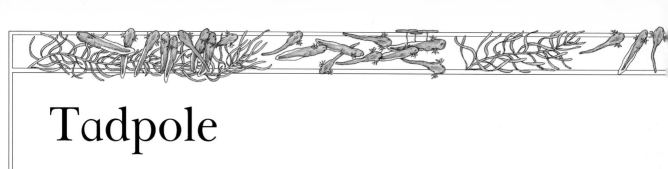

Tadpole

I am four weeks old now.
I like to swim with the
other tadpoles.

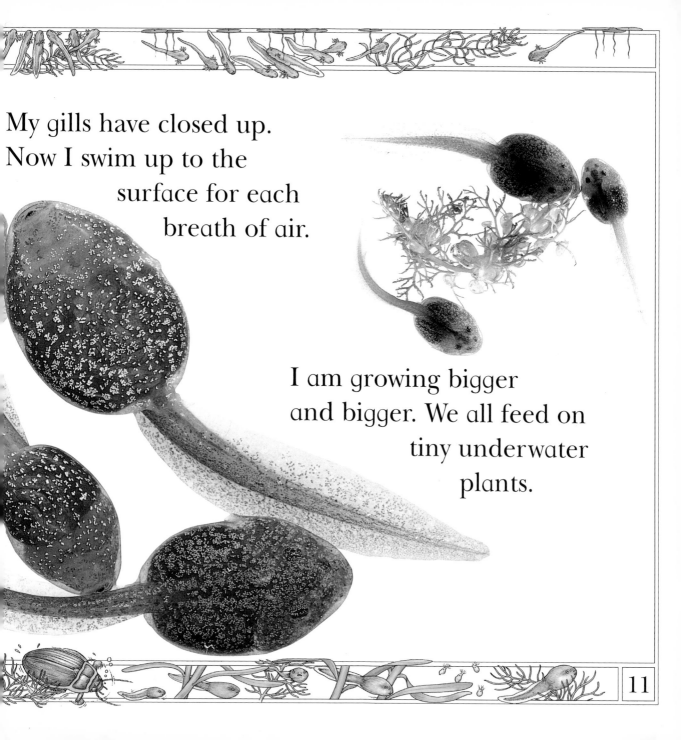

My gills have closed up.
Now I swim up to the
        surface for each
            breath of air.

I am growing bigger
and bigger. We all feed on
            tiny underwater
                plants.

Back legs first

I am six weeks old and I
have grown much bigger.
I eat plants and insects
that fall into the water.

I like to swim on my own now.
My back legs are beginning to grow.
I am slowly changing into a frog.

Frogpole

I am nine
weeks old. I
am half
tadpole and
half frog.

My back legs are
growing longer and now my
front legs are growing too.

A frog at last

I am nearly twelve weeks
old and I am a
frog at last.

I still have a long tail which
helps me swim, but it is
getting shorter.

Here is a really big frog. Look how small I am beside her!

Out of the water

Now I am more than one year old, and I spend most of my time on land.

I sit quietly watching
out for an insect to
eat. Then I shoot
out my long tongue
and snap it up.

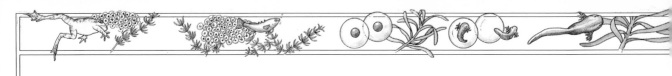

See how I grew

The egg   One day old   Four weeks old

Six weeks old   Nine weeks old

Over one year old

Twelve weeks old

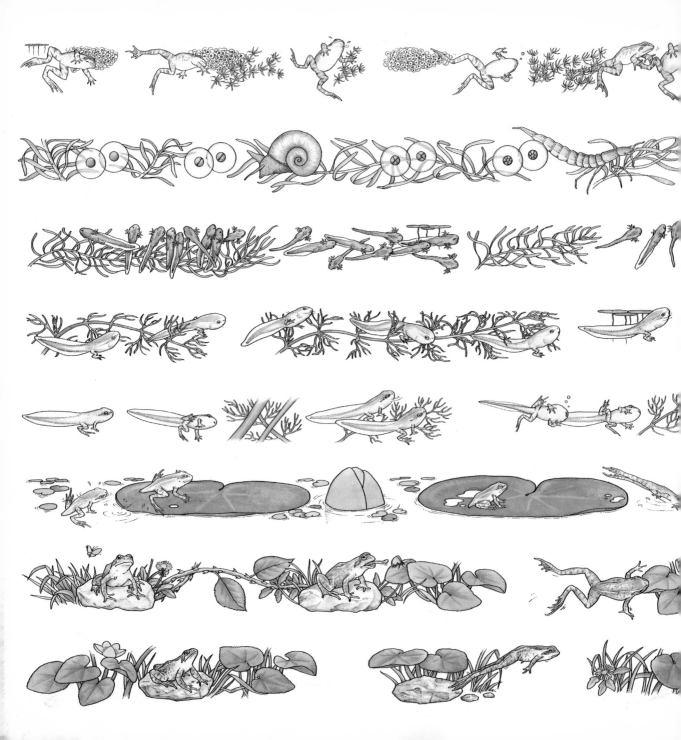

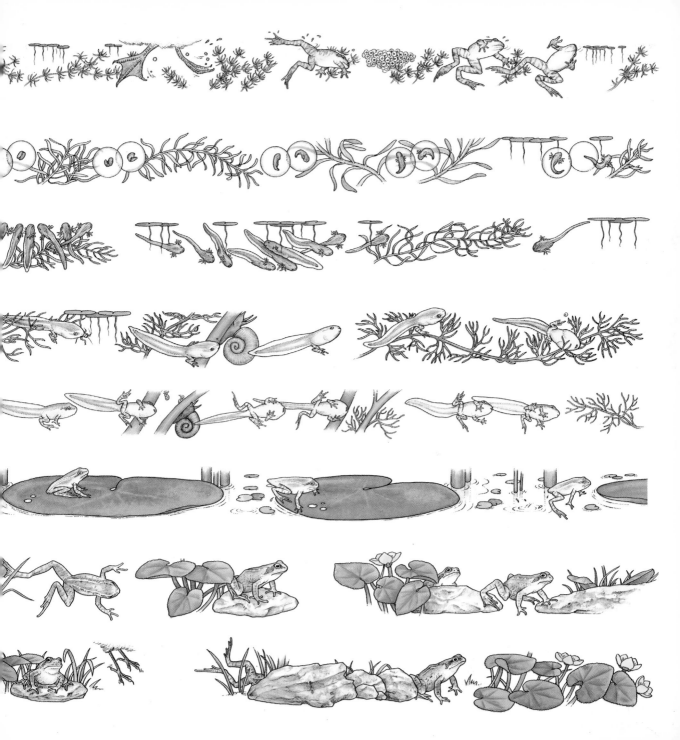